DEER HUNTER'S
Devotional

31 Days to Scout, Hunt & Harvest a Deeper Walk with God

By

Brad Duncan

Copyright © 2016 by Brad Duncan
All rights reserved

First Printing, 2016

Bradleyjeep Publishing
ISBN#978-0-9912858-6-0

Cover art by Tanner Ward
Copyright 2016

"Scripture quotations taken from the New American Standard Bible ® (NASB), Copyright © 1960, 1962, 1963, 1968, 1971, 1972, 1973, 1975, 1977, 1995 by the Lockman Foundation. Used by permission." (www.Lockman.org.)

Acknowledgments

I grew up hunting and fishing in southern Arkansas thanks to my dad, Ronnie Duncan. I learned early on from him that hunting and fishing was about a lot more than killing and catching. I've never met anyone who enjoys life more than him. Especially the hunting and fishing part of it! He makes everyone's trip better, and I'm proud he is my dad. Lots of other friends and family members made my trips fun and adventurous. I learned from them early in life to get outdoors and enjoy God's creation.

Thanks to my awesome wife, Michelle, for all of her support in writing this book and letting me get away to the woods without ever complaining.

Special thanks to Steve "Wildman" Wilson for his contributions to Arkansas wildlife and being kind enough to write the foreword to this devotional.

Foreword

God reveals himself to most of his people in three different ways; His word (the Bible), His spirit (Holy Spirit) and His creation (nature). As for me, nature speaks the loudest and clearest of the three. There is nothing more powerful to me than watching the woods come alive as the sun rises over the horizon…or the beauty of a whitetail deer feeding under an oak tree in the river bottoms…or the sound of a turkey gobble as he goes to roost for the evening. Many lessons of life are taught and learned while experiencing God's creation. This book shares just a few of the ways God reveals himself through times with family and friends in the outdoors. Some of my greatest memories are those with my family and friends at deer camp in south Arkansas, similar to those shared by Brad in this short book of devotionals---that is why I hope you look forward to reading these brief spiritual insights the next 31 days to "scout, hunt and harvest a deeper walk with God."

Steve "Wildman" Wilson

Prepare For the Journey

There's an old saying: "if you're too busy to go hunting, you're too busy." While this saying is true, the same idea can be applied to our spiritual lives. "If you're too busy to spend time with God, you're too busy."

There are several things to do when you prepare to go hunting. You must decide what area to hunt. Make sure your identification and hunting tags are current. Pack your weapons and ammo. I like to always have a watch, some water, and a flashlight in my backpack. These are some of the basics, but with each hunt and every hunter there are multiple accessories to choose from. When I prepare for a hunting trip in advance I get more out of the hunt. It's a miserable feeling to climb into your stand and realize you forgot your bullets!

In the same way, if you prepare to use this devotional you will get more from it. You can go through this individually or with a group. It's always best to spend a few minutes praying before you do anything. Just keep it simple and ask God to teach you what He wants you to know. Read the story, the scripture, and the questions. The questions are meant to help you think deeper about how the stories relate to you personally and how you might apply them to your life.

In the book of James in the Bible it says, "Draw near to God and He will draw near to you…" (James 4:8a). Take this opportunity to seek Jesus and you very well might harvest a treasure greater than you ever expected. May God bless you on your journey!

Day 1 – Light Overcomes the Darkness

The opening day of deer season in November 1983 couldn't come fast enough for me. While I had regularly gone rabbit hunting and fishing with my dad, he wouldn't take me deer hunting until he felt like I was old enough to hunt on my own. So each fall, when deer season would open, I would spend my Saturdays dreadfully shopping with my mom and dreaming about going to deer camp with my dad.

I got up early on that first cold morning and dressed in multiple layers of clothes. As I followed my dad through the woods, the beams from our flashlights pierced the pitch-black darkness. We arrived at my stand and I carefully climbed the frost-covered ladder. My dad handed me my 12 gauge shotgun, buckshot shells, and a Snickers candy bar. He reminded me that he would be back to pick me up and emphasized NOT to shoot him when he returned! Moments later his flashlight disappeared into the darkness. Suddenly, I began hearing crunching sounds all around me. As a thirteen-year-old, excitement and fear gripped me. I imagined deer, or possibly ferocious predators, all around. The darkened minutes slowly ticked away. Gradually, the sky above turned a lighter shade of grey. Light was breaking through the darkness. When I was finally able to see, I noticed a leaf from a big oak tree gently fall to the ground. When it landed it made a "crunching" sound. My herd of deer and ferocious beasts were simply leaves falling.

Spiritually, when we are in the dark, some things seem much better than they actually are. Other things seem much scarier. Only when the light overcomes the darkness are we able to truly recognize what the good or bad things are around us and inside of us. Are you living in the light of God's truth today?

"The Light shines in the darkness, and the darkness did not overpower it." John 1:5

Identify Your Target

🦌 Are there any areas the light has overcome the darkness in your life?

_____
_____
_____
_____
_____
_____
_____

Take Your Shot

🎯 What steps will you take this week to shine the light into the darkness around you?

_____
_____
_____
_____
_____
_____
_____

Day 2 – Buck Fever

I couldn't wait for the opening day of my second deer season in 1984. I hunted hard until about eight-thirty according to my Darth Vader watch. I decided to eat my Snickers. As I finished my frozen candy bar, I felt something looking at me. Somehow a spike had walked right underneath my stand! We stared at each other, both of us in shock. My shotgun was across my lap, my left hand was in place on the pump action, but my right hand held an empty Snickers wrapper. I had been taught not to make any sudden movements. Releasing the Snickers wrapper and only moving my right hand, I tried to find the safety and trigger without breaking my eye-contact with the spike. Not only could I not find the trigger, but I realized that my heart was beating like crazy and that I couldn't breathe. I felt my right hand touching my left, which was still on the pump action. I had slid my right hand all the way up the gun barrel. I finally broke my gaze from the spike and moved my hand down and finger to the trigger. He trotted off about fifteen yards and stood broadside looking at me. (Spikes are so dumb – a lot like teenage boys!) I tried to control my breathing and raise my gun, but I could hardly move. As the deer trotted off, I finally threw my gun up, but it was too late to shoot. I spent the next several minutes shaking uncontrollably and wondering what had just happened.

Spiritually there are times when God places us in situations where we feel like we're in shock. Someone asks us about our faith, asks us to pray in public, or to give our testimony, and we go blank. Later we think, "I should have said this" or "I should have done that". Begin preparing today to be able to share what you believe and why you believe it.

"...sanctify Christ as Lord in your hearts, always being ready to make a defense to everyone who asks you to give an account for the hope that is in you, yet with gentleness and reverence." 1 Peter 3:15

Identify Your Target

Can you think of a situation where you wish you had been better equipped spiritually?

_____
_____
_____
_____
_____
_____
_____

Take Your Shot

What did you learn from that situation to be better prepared in the future?

_____
_____
_____
_____
_____
_____
_____

Day 3 – Powder, Patch, Ball

When we began hunting with muzzleloaders in the late 1980's it was a whole new ballgame. I knew something was weird when I saw my dad loading up black powder, white patches and metal balls into an old orange purse of my grandma's. He and my Uncle Jerry were laughing like crazy about their new "hunting accessories." One phrase that became popular with muzzle loading was "powder, patch, ball." Guys would laugh and talk while loading their muskets, and eventually someone would get caught holding their metal ball in their hand wondering if they had put powder in already. Another guy would laughingly say, "powder, patch, ball!"

With advances in muzzleloader technology, it's rare to misfire or load your gun wrong these days. But we still joke around when loading our pyrodex powder pellets and sabot bullets saying, "powder, patch, ball."

God gives us practical advice to live by in the Bible. While some things can be confusing, the basic story of the Bible is simple. God created people. People sinned. God sent his Son, Jesus, to take the punishment for our sin. If we repent and follow Him we will be saved from our sin.

Acknowledge Jesus as Lord and begin following Him right now. Be baptized. And then, in His power, begin doing the things He wants you to do.

"If anyone serves Me, he must follow Me; and where I am, there My servant will be also; if anyone serves Me, the Father will honor him."
John 12:26

Identify Your Target

Do you have things spiritually in order in your life?

_____
_____
_____
_____
_____
_____
_____

Take Your Shot

What do you need to do to grow spiritually today?

_____
_____
_____
_____
_____
_____
_____
_____

Day 4 – Unplugged

In 1984 my dad and about fifteen other men decided to start their own deer camp. They took an old tin cow barn, poured a concrete floor in it, and hooked up electricity. A 55-gallon barrel was converted into a wood-burning stove. Bunk beds were added and soon the barn was renovated into a great deer camp. We didn't have TV there. No cell phones or internet either. We spent our evenings playing darts and listening to whatever random south Arkansas high school football game we could pick up on the radio. Those were some of the best times of laughter and competition. If we went into town to check a deer or get ice we would call home on a pay phone and update moms, wives, and girlfriends on who had killed what.

Today things have changed so much. We now have a satellite dish hanging on the side of our old tin barn. Although the cell phone signal isn't great, you can check your email, fantasy football team, or Facebook in camp or on your deer stand. It's convenient, but I'm glad I grew up in a time when we had to unplug and enjoy life with the people who were in the room. I learned so much about being a man from watching and listening to those guys.

Modern technology is fantastic, but I believe it can lead us to miss some of the greatest things in life...other people. Relationships with our spouses, kids, families, and friends can be hindered if we are more connected to cyberspace than to them. In fact, God specifically tells us to be still and know that he is God. When we spend so much time entertaining ourselves we are in danger of missing the best things in this life: real relationships with God and other people.

"Cease striving and know that I am God; I will be exalted among the nations, I will be exalted in the earth." Psalms 46:10

Identify Your Target

Has technology or entertainment stolen time from your relationships with God, family, or friends?

_____
_____
_____
_____
_____
_____
_____

Take Your Shot

How will you reclaim some time to develop and enjoy those relationships?

_____
_____
_____
_____
_____
_____
_____
_____

Day 5 – It's a Trap!

During rifle season, many guys in our deer camp would put on their best camo clothes and go to a small church on Sundays. Back in the 80's, deer scent covers were a whole new idea. The first scent cover I can remember was worn by Jim Holloway, who had a small canister of skunk scent clipped onto his hat. One Sunday, he wore that hat with the scent canister on it to church. About ten minutes into the service our eyes started watering, because the skunk smell from that canister was seeping out. A guy leaned over and told him what was happening. Jim laughingly asked, "Do you want me to open the vent on it?"

Deer scents and covers have grown exponentially since then. According to the U.S. Fish and Wildlife Service, Americans spend over $39 billion dollars annually on everything from camouflage clothes, scent killers, deer calls, doe urine, and other equipment. All in an effort to fool a deer into thinking this area of woods is a great place to visit, let your guard down, and have some fun! But the reality is that it's a trap, and can cost a deer its life.

We have an enemy, Satan, who also sets traps for us. We have to stay alert. The Bible teaches us practical ways to avoid the snares of our enemy. Many times Satan tells you this will be a great place to visit, let your guard down, and have some fun. But it could be a trap, and could cost you your life. Staying in fellowship with God will help you avoid things that sound good, but that eventually lead to misery or even death.

"Put on the full armor of God, so that you will be able to stand firm against the schemes of the devil." Ephesians 6:11

Identify Your Target

What are some traps men fall into? Are you in danger of falling into any of these?

_____
_____
_____
_____
_____
_____
_____
_____

Take Your Shot

What will you do to avoid these snares? How can you help set other men free from these traps?

_____
_____
_____
_____
_____
_____
_____
_____

Day 6 – *A Priceless Heirloom...Or Not*

When we formed our deer camp in 1984 members donated all kinds of furniture and appliances to use. Someone brought a picnic table. Another person gave us a huge gun rack. Jerry Riddle brought his grandmother's kitchen table and chairs. One morning it was freezing outside and I came in to eat and warm up. We had converted a 55 gallon drum into a wood burning stove. As my dad and I ate breakfast with Phil Ericson we were freezing because we had run out of wood. All of the trees outside were frozen solid, covered in thick ice. My dad leaned back in his chair and it made a creaking sound. He said, "This chair isn't safe." Then he stood up, grabbed the chair, and lifted it up in the air, seemingly to inspect it. A moment later he slammed the chair onto the concrete floor, busting it to pieces. He smiled and proclaimed, "Looks like we have some wood!" We laughed and over the next couple of hours fed the kitchen table and chairs into the wood burning stove. Around noon, Jerry walked in from hunting. He looked around curiously for his grandma's table. Before too long he noticed the last broken chair leg by the stove. He asked, "Where's my grandma's table." Realizing Jerry wasn't happy about the situation my dad said, "Jerry, your grandma saved our lives." Jerry didn't think it was funny, but everyone else thought it was hilarious!

Some things are important to you, but not to others. Ultimately all of our possessions will be gone. The only things we will have are the treasures we store in heaven. One of the greatest things you can take to heaven is other people. God calls us to share the gospel with others. He does the saving, but He allows us the blessing of being part of His incredible plan.

DEER HUNTER'S DEVOTIONAL

"Therefore, we are ambassadors for Christ, as though God were making an appeal through us; we beg you on behalf of Christ, be reconciled to God." 2 Corinthians 5:20

Identify Your Target

Do you spend any time really thinking about eternity?

_____
_____
_____
_____
_____
_____
_____

Take Your Shot

What steps will you take to store up treasures in heaven?

_____
_____
_____
_____
_____
_____
_____
_____

Day 7 – *Tell Me That Old, Old Story*

When I was a kid I was mesmerized by the stories my dad and his friends told about deer camp. There was the time when Tommy Lewis was walking to his deer stand at daybreak and killed a huge buck. Another time my dad and uncle put up a deer stand, then walked about 400 yards and put up another one. The next morning, Dad got into his stand and watched Uncle Jerry's flashlight slowly go away into the darkness. A few minutes later a flashlight was coming back from another direction. The light stopped about 50 yards away from my dad. At dawn my dad and uncle could wave at each other from their stands. I could sit and listen to these men tell of their victories, failures, and mishaps for hours. Hearing them helped shape my idea of what deer hunting was really all about. I learned how to speak the language, what things you should and shouldn't do to be a successful hunter, and that even though you don't always come back with a big buck, you seldom return from hunting without some great memories.

I wonder how many boys get to hear stories of the victories, failures, and mishaps men have had in their Christian walk. I am fortunate to have been raised around mature, Godly men who shared their stories of faith with me. Their adventures inspire me. It's important to share the stories of your walk with God. Hearing Christian men's adventures helps to shape a boy's mind into what being a man is really all about. They learn how to speak the language, what things they should and shouldn't do to be a successful Christian, and that even though you don't always have immediate success, you seldom return from time following God without some great memories. It's vital that followers of Christ share their stories with others.

"One generation shall praise Your works to another, and shall declare Your mighty acts." Psalms 145:4

Identify Your Target

Growing up did you have anyone who shared stories about the greatness of God with you?

_____
_____
_____
_____
_____
_____
_____
_____

Take Your Shot

Who will you share your experiences of God with this week?

_____
_____
_____
_____
_____
_____
_____
_____
_____

Day 8 – Lost!

I was 17 years old and headed out with my rifle early one morning to walk about 100 yards to hunt the Pump stand near our camp. Tom Beary pulled up to me on his dirt bike and asked where I was going to hunt. After I told him, he asked why I wasn't going to the new stand over by the power line. There were fresh rubs and scrapes all around it. Excited, I hopped on the back of his cycle, agreeing to let him take me over there. We rode over to the power line and drove down it to the third hill. Tom stopped and let me off. He told me to walk in about 75 yards and that I couldn't miss the stand. I began walking into the woods and it kept getting thicker and thicker. I decided to walk back to the power line. After walking for several minutes I realized I was completely lost. I began telling myself to calm down and focus. I distinctly remember sitting down and eating a candy bar thinking this might be the last thing I ate for a very long time. After resting and gathering myself, I moved through the woods and came across a distinct four-wheeler trail. My heart leapt knowing this would eventually take me out of the woods. After a long walk, I finally made it home. When I walked back into camp Tom was sitting at the kitchen table with some other guys eating breakfast. After telling my story a guy said, "That stand is off the second hill, not the third." Tom belly laughed and said, "Oops!"

Many times in life you think you're going in the right direction and before you know it you're lost. You lose a job, someone important to you passes away, a relationship ends, or numerous other things can make you feel lost. Life is confusing sometimes. God created you for a purpose. He wants to lead you out of the wilderness back home.

"For the Son of Man has come to seek and to save that which was lost."
Luke 19:10

Identify Your Target

Have you ever been lost physically or spiritually?

___

Take Your Shot

If you are currently lost, what can you do to get back on track? If you're not lost is there someone you can help to find their way?

___

Day 9 – Getting Wet Isn't Always Getting Baptized

In the years before we had a dependable water supply at the camp we transported 55-gallon barrels of water from town. My Uncle Jerry had rigged up a RV pump so we would have running water. Some people called it ingenious, while others called it "redneck engineering." Either way we were just happy to have running water. One night Phil Ericson, Uncle Jerry, and my dad made a run to town to get water. On the way home, with no guns in the truck, they were driving down an old oil road and spotlighting the woods looking for deer. As they began going down a steep hill my dad yelled, "Deer!" Phil slammed on the breaks causing the 55 gallon barrels to suddenly slide forward, shattering the back glass and pouring a tidal-wave of water into the cab all over them. A few seconds later completely wet and with broken glass all over them my dad said, "I'm still on the deer."

Many people have chosen not to be baptized for a multitude of reasons: they are embarrassed, their parents didn't encourage it, or they didn't realize its importance. Other people have been baptized, but it was before they were truly saved. They got baptized because they were pressured to early in life, or they did it to please someone. If you haven't been baptized or your baptism is out of Biblical order, it's easy to fix. Like a pastor I know once said, "If you get baptized and aren't saved, you are simply getting wet."

"He who has believed and has been baptized shall be saved; but he who has disbelieved shall be condemned." Mark 16:16

Identify Your Target

Have you been baptized since you've been saved?

_____
_____
_____
_____
_____
_____
_____

Take Your Shot

If you haven't been baptized talk to your pastor or Christian friend about it today.

_____
_____
_____
_____
_____
_____
_____
_____

Day 10 – *You Won't Know If You Don't Go*

When I was young I'd ask my Dad: "Do you think the deer are moving in this rain? This wind? This heat?" My Dad came up with a reply to all my questions about the possibility of getting a deer with the saying, "You won't know if you don't go."

One Thanksgiving weekend hunt we had 30 mph winds. Several guys slept in that morning because of the bad weather. My dad and I were hunting in stands near one another. He had his new Remington .270 rifle sitting across his lap. Amazingly, a few hours into the hunt two doe came walking down the trail straight toward him in the strong wind. He excitedly reached down for his gun, and accidentally pulled the trigger with the gun still in his lap! The deer ran away from him and straight to me. Thanks to my dad I got the only deer taken that weekend!

You can have success in good and bad conditions. Just because conditions aren't optimal doesn't mean you shouldn't go hunting.

Spiritually, there are times in our lives when we don't think conditions are ideal to share our faith. There may be a family member, friend, or coworker who doesn't seem have any interest in hearing about your relationship with God. One time I absolutely did not want to share my faith with a coworker. We were different socially and racially, but I knew God wanted me to talk to him about my faith. I was amazed at how he began asking me questions about my belief in Jesus. A short time later, I had the honor of praying with him for Salvation. About a week later, I had the blessing of baptizing him. God took a situation that I saw as hopeless and a waste of time and taught me to be obedient to Him.

"The wind blows where it wishes and you hear the sound of it, but do not know where it comes from and where it is going; so is everyone who is born of the Spirit." John 3:8

Identify Your Target

Has God ever led you to do something that made you uncomfortable?

_____
_____
_____
_____
_____
_____
_____
_____

Take Your Shot

What can you do this week to step out of your comfort zone and share Jesus with someone?

_____
_____
_____
_____
_____
_____
_____
_____

Day 11 – You Can't Get a Big One If You're Busy Skinnin' the Little Ones

In 2004, I was rifle hunting when I saw movement over to my left. Through the woods I saw a nice doe coming toward me. She stopped perfectly in an opening between some trees. The thought crossed my mind to take her immediately, but I reasoned that the bucks were in rut and if I waited I might see a bigger deer. A few seconds later a nine-point buck stepped into the picture just behind her. He gave her a little nudge on her backside with his rack. I got my crosshairs on him quickly and went from having a doe to having a trophy buck. Hunters have different goals. Some just want meat in the freezer. Others want to tag as many deer as possible. Still others want to get a wall-hanger. If your goal is to get a big buck, a lot of times you have to pass up the smaller deer to see the big one.

One of our biggest enemies in serving God is being too busy. I've heard it said, "If Satan can't make you bad, he'll make you busy." The early church struggled with this and we still do today. It's easy to get busy doing good things and miss out on doing the great things God created you to do. Be careful to know your purpose, pass on the things that get in the way of it, and set your aim on the correct target. Sometimes saying, "No", is the best thing you can do in your spiritual and hunting journey.

"Therefore be careful how you walk, not as unwise men but as wise, making the most of your time, because the days are evil. So then do not be foolish, but understand what the will of the Lord is." Ephesians 5:15-17

Identify Your Target

Are you focused on how you should be serving Jesus today?

_____
_____
_____
_____
_____
_____
_____
_____

Take Your Shot

Is there anything you need to start doing or stop doing to follow the Lord more closely?

_____
_____
_____
_____
_____
_____
_____
_____

Day 12 - *The Joy Is In the Journey*

It was Friday afternoon the day before the opening of muzzle-loading season. Several guys were bow-hunting that day as a bonus hunt. My dad was fortunate enough to stick a deer well before dark, but he couldn't find it. He came back to camp and gathered me, Uncle Jerry, Kevin Martin, and my cousin, Tyge. We jumped on our four-wheelers and headed over to help him look for it. On the way my dad showed us a tree filled with buckeyes and we each grabbed one. After finding some blood and trailing it about seventy-five yards the blood-trail stopped. We gathered around and jokingly took our buckeyes out and rubbed them for luck. Spreading out to look again Tyge yelled, "Got him!" We loaded up my dad's first "bow-kill" and celebrated all the way back to camp. As we cleaned his deer, we took turns telling our version of the story and laughing about our lucky buckeyes.

Deer hunting is a lot of work and yet "work" is not the word used when describing it. Building deer stands, cutting shooting lanes, and walking miles through the woods to find just the right place to put a deer stand are a few of the things that will wear you completely out. Pulling the trigger is often the easiest part of getting a deer. Many times you have to trail the deer, then drag it out, clean it, and process it. All of this is done with guys helping and laughing as everyone shares stories of success and failures they've experienced.

In the same way, our "work" at church should be such a journey. As we clean the church grounds, serve others, and go about doing ministry we should have a joy about us. Has church become a burden? Hard work might be part of it, but it should be a joyful journey.

"There is nothing better for a man than to eat and drink and tell himself that his labor is good. This also I have seen that it is from the hand of God." Ecclesiastes 2:24

Identify Your Target

List something you have done in service to God that was hard work but was enjoyable.

_____
_____
_____
_____
_____
_____
_____

Take Your Shot

Look for some ways this week to serve your church or other people and be intentional about enjoying it.

_____
_____
_____
_____
_____
_____
_____

Day 13 – Wanderlust

Hunters and hunting agencies are responsible for the deer herd resurgence in the past 20-30 years. Through money spent on hunting licenses and applying responsible hunting regulations the dismal deer herd in my home state of Arkansas has grown tremendously over the past few decades. Modern gun deer hunting is scheduled around a time known as the rut. Early and late ruts are the two times of the year when bucks, young and old, lose their minds. The careful life a mature buck leads is shown by his longevity. If a buck lives past his fourth year he has a very high chance of dying of natural causes. The others usually are taken during the ten-to-fourteen day rut. As the doe come into heat the bucks' necks begin to swell, their hormones ramp up, and they go looking for love – BIG TIME! Controlled by their hormones they mark their areas with scrapes and rubs, fight other bucks for breeding dominance, and basically live for sex. With their minds fixed on this they become vulnerable.

Men are a lot like this, but for more than ten to fourteen days a year. When we focus on lust we lose our focus on God. He provides sex for us to enjoy in a healthy relationship with a woman to whom we're committed in marriage. If we don't control our thoughts and urges then we become vulnerable to the attacks of our enemy.

"We are destroying speculations and every lofty thing raised up against the knowledge of God, and we are taking every thought captive to the obedience of Christ." 2 Corinthians 10:5

<u>*Identify Your Target*</u>

Do you keep your thoughts in check? Do you struggle with lust or pornography?

_____
_____
_____
_____
_____
_____
_____
_____

<u>*Take Your Shot*</u>

- Pray that God will help you overcome this sin and recruit another Christian man to help you win by keeping you accountable.

_____
_____
_____
_____
_____
_____
_____
_____

Day 14 – *Outmaneuvered*

My grandpa would have never been accused of being a great deer hunter. When he was young, going deer hunting consisted mainly of sitting around a camp fire and listening to the dogs run. One time when he was older and not in good health, he took a lawn chair out into the woods and wandered around until he found a spot to hunt. Turns out he sat right under a friend of ours, Larry Wilson, who was in a climber stand. Larry whistled and whispered until he got my grandpa's attention. To Larry's amazement, Grandpa simply waved at him and went back to hunting. On another day Grandpa came back from hunting and said he had seen a buck. When asked why he didn't shoot it he answered in his slow southern drawl, "Well boys, he outmaneuvered me." We laughed until we hurt.

If you've hunted much you've probably experienced being outmaneuvered. I can't tell you how many times I've thought while hunting: "One more step and I'll have a shot; wait! Where did he go?" Deer are unpredictable and things rarely ever go exactly as planned.

Our spiritual life can be the same way. You see a great way to serve God and things don't go as you planned. You do everything you know to do and God goes left instead of right. You step out in faith and things don't go anything like you expected.

God is faithful, but He doesn't always work the way we want him to. Most of the people God has used for His glory didn't understand their situations until after the fact and sometimes never in this life. But God is faithful and ultimately everything will make perfect sense.

"For My thoughts are not your thoughts, nor are your ways My ways,' declares the Lord." Isaiah 55:8

Identify Your Target

Has God ever worked in ways you didn't understand?

Take Your Shot

Ask Him to allow you to see why, but even if he doesn't, ask Him to heal your hurts.

Day 15 – Hunter or Hunted

Early one morning Kevin Martin and I took off on our four-wheelers in the dark and made our way deep into the woods. The stands we were hunting from were a few hundred yards apart so we parked at a fork in the road to split up. We grabbed our bows and told each other, "Good luck." I had my flashlight and walked in my hunting boots at a slow pace. I still had plenty of time before daylight. About 50 yards down the trail from where we parked, a pack of coyotes broke the silence of my early morning walk with their terrifying yelping! They were close and I only had a bow. I had begun this walk as the hunter. Now, I was the hunted. Needless to say my pace picked up greatly. With my heart racing I didn't hesitate scaling the ladder of my deer stand when I reached it. After settling down and taking a deep breath I gripped my bow and said defiantly, "Come on by now!"

In the real world predators can become prey in a snap. And just as quickly they can turn back into the predators. There are dangers out there. I've learned that when I'm in the woods I have to be prepared to protect myself from things that might do me harm.

Spiritually we encounter the same thing. We can simply be driving to work when someone cuts us off in traffic. If we're not careful this anger can escalate into a rage. We can let our mouths run without thinking and that can lead to bad situations. A flirtation online can lead to sexual indiscretions in the real world. Satan can, and will, use seemingly safe, everyday situations to get our minds off God. We must intentionally focus on Jesus or we may be devoured!

"Be of sober spirit, be on the alert. Your adversary, the devil, prowls around like a roaring lion, seeking someone to devour."
1 Peter 5:8

Identify Your Target

Are there areas in your life where you are not on alert?

_____
_____
_____
_____
_____
_____
_____
_____

Take Your Shot

Ask God to point out any possible situations where you might be vulnerable and adjust your habits to defend yourself.

_____
_____
_____
_____
_____
_____
_____
_____
_____

Day 16 – Bullseye

I was a skinny ten-year-old kid the first time I got to shoot my dad's deer rifle. He had a Marlin .35 caliber rifle with a 3x9 Tasco scope. It took everything I had to hold that gun up and try to keep it on the target. Dad told me to put the crosshairs on the bullseye and gently squeeze the trigger. I held the gun up, but I was too weak to hold it in place. It moved back and forth over the target several times. Finally, I anticipated crossing the bullseye and pulled the trigger! An explosion rang out! I quickly realized my dad had failed to tell me one important thing: don't put the scope directly against your eye!

On a positive note, I got to brag for several days about how I got such a big black eye.

When sighting in a scope there are vertical and horizontal crosshairs. Both have to be on to hit your target. One time, I shot a muzzleloader literally 22 times before I got it sighted in. I'm surprised the barrel didn't melt! I realized at about shot number 17 the barrel had to be swabbed out after each shot for that particular gun to shoot true.

Jesus teaches us that our vertical relationship with God and our horizontal relationships with people are the two most important things in this life. When we get those two things right we can hit the bullseye of our purpose here in this world. Sometimes we feel like we love people, but not God. Other times we love God, but not people. Jesus says we must love God and people if we are to hit the mark.

"And he answered, 'You shall love the Lord your God with all your heart, and with all your soul, and with all your strength, and with all your mind; and your neighbor as yourself.'" Luke 10:27

Identify Your Target

Do you have a love for Jesus and for His people?

_____
_____
_____
_____
_____
_____
_____

Take Your Shot

What are some ways you can show God's love by sacrificing for others this week?

_____
_____
_____
_____
_____
_____
_____

Day 17 – Permanent Stand - Not So Permanent

For several years we hunted predominately out of ladder stands that were fairly easy to move from one place to another. And we moved them regularly. Almost every afternoon during deer season at least one stand would be moved. One location turned out to be very productive. My dad killed several deer from there. I distinctly remember one cold morning watching a doe lead her fawn down the stream that ran by this stand. They never knew I was there and it was so enjoyable watching them move silently through the woods.

Tom Beary had shot at a big buck with a bow out of this particular ladder stand. The deer was about fifteen yards away, but a tree was only fourteen yards away! He hit the tree dead center. Later, we cut the tree down, broad head intact, and made Tom a plaque with it that read "Tree-rific Shot" to hang up in his office.

This area was so productive my dad said he was going to build a "permanent stand that would always be there." We built the huge permanent box stand, but within five years the area was clear cut and not hunted anymore. We recently found the stand in the overgrown thicket. It's now rotten and has a family of raccoons living in it. So much for its permanency.

Many things in the world are a lot like this. We think something is permanent, but over time it can change. A marriage fails, a loved one dies, or a job ends. Jesus teaches that the things of this world will all pass away, but His Word and His people will last forever.

"The world is passing away, and also its lusts; but the one who does the will of God lives forever." 1 John 2:17

Identify Your Target

Think of something you considered permanent in your life that turned out not to be so.

_____
_____
_____
_____
_____
_____
_____

Take Your Shot

How can you begin to place your priorities in things that will last forever?

_____
_____
_____
_____
_____
_____
_____

Day 18 – Gentlemen's Agreement

In May of 1996 my cousin, Tyge, suggested we implement a "three point rule". This had increased the overall quality of bucks tremendously in other camps. Everyone got excited hearing about having larger bucks and agreed to the rule in our camp. Instead of imposing a fine for breaking the rule we decided to just go with a "gentleman's agreement."

By December of that hunting season many people had passed spikes and young, forked-horn bucks. It was tough, because in those days it was rare to see a quality buck in south Arkansas. We don't hunt with dogs, but my dad was hunting when a random dog got hot on the trail of something. It came closer and closer when all of a sudden a deer burst onto the scene in a full sprint. Dad threw his rifle up and dropped the running deer. He climbed down and walked over to find it was a spike! He thought to himself, "No one's going to care after I tell them about the incredible shot I just made." How wrong he was. Tyge, his nephew, jumped on him immediately when he got back to camp. When Dad kept celebrating his shot, Tyge began griping at Tom Beary who asked, "Why are you getting onto me?" Tyge answered, "Because Uncle Ronnie doesn't care!"

It didn't take long for another member to kill a spike and the rule was thrown out. Dad just laughed and said, "I guess I'm not a gentleman; but you wouldn't care if you would have seen the shot I made!"

Spiritually there are many times when we know the right thing to do, but in the heat of the moment we choose to ignore it. We have to prepare to follow God even when there are temptations that make us want to do things we shouldn't.

"For what I am doing, I do not understand; for I am not practicing what I would like to do, but I am doing the very thing I hate." Romans 7:15

Identify Your Target

Have you been in a situation where you didn't intend to sin, but were in the middle of it before you realized it?

_____
_____
_____
_____
_____
_____
_____
_____

Take Your Shot

What steps will you take to avoid falling into sin again?

_____
_____
_____
_____
_____
_____
_____
_____
_____

Day 19 – Dress for Success

Deer can move at all hours during the day and night. Some guys are known to get up super-early and get out there well before dawn. Others have a reputation of sleeping in and then rushing to their stands just as the sun is rising. One guy in our camp, John Honea, gets up early, leisurely drinks his coffee, and still gets out to his stand before daylight. One particular morning he had followed this same routine and headed out to his stand in the early darkness. A little while later my dad took off on his four-wheeler just as it was getting daylight. He ran across John who was heading back to camp. Dad pulled up and asked him, "Did you forget something?"

John answered, "Well, when I got to my stand and got off my wheeler I realized I had these on!"

Dad looked over at John and saw along with his mossy oak camo hunting jacket and pants he had on his house shoes!

Dad started laughing and John just shook his head in disgust.

In the Bible, Paul instructs followers of Jesus to put on armor for spiritual battle. A helmet, sword, breastplate, belt, shield, and even footwear are listed as items to protect us from the flaming arrows of Satan. Every person deals with different temptations, but we all have struggles in this life to face.

Paul also says that our spiritual battle isn't against physical enemies, but against the spiritual forces of evil in the heavenly realms.

If you put on the correct armor spiritually you'll be prepared to fight the good fight. If you put on the correct footwear when hunting, you'll get to be in your stand before daylight.

"For our struggle is not against flesh and blood, but against the rulers, against the powers, against the world forces of this darkness, against the spiritual forces of wickedness in the heavenly places." Ephesians 6:12

Identify Your Target

Do you ever think about the spiritual battles going on all around you?

Take Your Shot

Think of some ways you can prepare to fight the spiritual battles you face every day.

Day 20 – Redemption

Fortunately, I was able to harvest a spike on the opening morning of the 1997 season. Unfortunately, I shot it really high and with the help of several guys had to blood-trail it for hours through a thicket. We got back into camp with my deer around noon. After eating some lunch, cleaning my deer, and sharing stories from the morning's hunt, I wanted to go back out. Until that time I had only killed spikes and doe, and wanted to kill a big buck. My Uncle Jerry had killed a five-point that morning on a new stand he was hunting from. I asked him if he was going back out and he said he wasn't.

I got into his stand about 3:30 that afternoon. I was happy to already have a deer tagged and was just enjoying relaxing. At 4:20 I looked down the hill to my left, and to my surprise, there stood a big buck with a nice rack eating acorns. This was the first deer with a rack I had ever seen. I caught my breath and slowly raised my gun. Getting on his front right shoulder, I squeezed the trigger. Boom! My shot rang out, but the buck just stood there. Then he put his head back down and ate another acorn! I put my scope back on him, steadied my gun and fired again. He immediately dropped. I kept my gun on him for ten minutes, then climbed down to ground check him. He was a nice eight point with a 14 1/2 inch spread. Everyone was happy for me, but amazed by my story. I realized that day I had been letting my rifle kick back, and that's why I was shooting high. I never had that problem again.

In life we don't always get a second chance. But when we mess up, it is a great opportunity to learn from our mistakes. I'm thankful Jesus uses our mistakes to teach us. Take inventory of yourself and adjust your actions to glorify God.

"Brethren, I do not regard myself as having laid hold of it yet; but one thing I do: forgetting what lies behind and reaching forward to what lies ahead, I press on toward the goal for the prize of the upward call of God in Christ Jesus." Philippians 3:13-14

Identify Your Target

Have you ever made a mistake that you learned from?

Take Your Shot

Who can you share your wisdom from your mistakes with this week?

Day 21 – Busted!

My alarm went off well before daylight. Like most mornings at deer camp, I climbed out of my warm bed and began the ritual of putting on layers of clothes. I ate a light breakfast with everyone and finished putting on my final layers of clothing, along with my hunter orange vest and cap. I climbed on my four-wheeler and made the cold drive back into the woods. On my walk into my stand I put out my cover scent. Climbing up into the stand I was careful to be as quiet as possible. I sat down and set up my gear. Extra shells, deer grunt, and backpack well within reach.

I settled in and waited for morning to arrive. A little while later birds were singing and squirrels were playing in the sunshine. I stealthily watched the woods for any trace of a deer moving through the area. Deer are sneaky. Sometimes they just appear in front of you and leave you wondering how they got that close without making a sound. Around mid-morning I heard something to my left. Without thinking, I let my guard down and quickly turned my head. A deer blew loudly at me breaking the silence of the woods. My eyes caught just a glimpse of it bounding away. Busted! All of my sacrifice getting out there early, putting out scent cover and waiting patiently was all wasted in a moment, because I let my guard down.

We can ruin our witness spiritually in a moment of letting our guard down as well. Losing our temper at work or in public over something insignificant can ruin our testimony about our Savior. A moment of letting our guard down can cost us our integrity. Be alert!

"Be on the alert, stand firm in the faith, act like men, be strong."
1 Corinthians 16:13

Identify Your Target

Do you lose your cool on a regular basis?

___

Take Your Shot

How can you learn to control your anger or help other men realize how important it is to control their anger?

___

DEER HUNTER'S DEVOTIONAL

Day 22 – Cadillac's Slogan (1959): "In a Realm All Its Own...Cadillac"

When Jerry Riddle's brother-in-law drove his new Cadillac to deer camp in the late 1980's the last thing he expected was to use it to haul a deer out of the woods. Pulling back into the woods the dirt road was muddy, but felt solid enough. They drove down to where they could park and walk to their stands. As luck would have it, Zach, Jerry's nephew, killed a spike. Then the adventure began. After much thought they decided to tie the deer to the top of the Cadillac's trunk. This weighed the car down and they sank into a mud hole trying to get back out to the paved road. After a few mild attempts to get out they decided they were stuck. My dad and Uncle Jerry ran across them and they explained their dilemma. My dad said, "No problem." He's never been one to go easy on a vehicle. He got behind the wheel and gunned it! It eventually got traction and he splashed through the mud. They drove back to camp with their prize deer on top of the Caddy.

Sometimes we do unorthodox things when we're deer hunting. God calls us to think outside of the box spiritually sometimes as well. I've seen a men's group meet on Saturday nights just to pray together. A youth group would meet at midnight on Friday night to read the Bible out loud for an hour. Another group of men chose to meet at 5 a.m. on Tuesdays to go through a devotional. All of these unique ideas led to a closer walk with God.

God might want you to lead a men's group, call someone and encourage them, or give up a TV show to spend some extra time in prayer. Just because it's a different way to do things doesn't mean it shouldn't be done.

"Trust in the Lord with all your heart, and do not lean on your own understanding. In all your ways acknowledge Him, and He will make your paths straight." Proverbs 3:5-6

Identify Your Target

Has God ever called you to do something outside of your comfort zone?

_____
_____
_____
_____
_____
_____
_____
_____

Take Your Shot

Is the Holy Spirit leading you to do anything that might take some extra courage?

_____
_____
_____
_____
_____
_____
_____
_____

Day 23 – I No Speaka the Language

If you are around deer hunters very long at all you quickly realize they have their own language. "There's fresh scrapes and rubs along the east fence line by the Double Ugly stand." What? "I saw a non-typical chasing a slick head across the creek from the Paradise stand." Huh? "I was gruntin', bleatin', and rattlin' at a wall-hanger, but when I dropped him there was a lot of ground shrinkage." Please explain.

This doesn't even touch the vocabulary of muzzle-loading which my mom won't allow my dad to use around her. Balls, nipples, nipple-pullers, and ram-rods are just a few of the terms guys love to run with when black-powder season is here. If you don't understand the language you'll be lost and confused in these conversations.

Many Christians have their own vocabulary too. Some phrases can freak out a person who doesn't speak the church lingo: "You need to be washed in the blood of the Lamb; I'm surrounded by an Angelic hedge of protection; We will now be drinking the blood and eating the flesh of Jesus!" These might be great things if you understand what they mean. But to those who don't, they can sound pretty crazy. If others don't understand the language they'll be lost and confused in these conversations. When you are sharing your faith be careful to speak in terms the people you are talking to can understand.

"So also you, unless you utter by the tongue speech that is clear, how will it be known what is spoken? For you will be speaking into the air."
1 Corinthians 14:9

Identify Your Target

Do you know people who overly use church language in ways that confuse others?

_____
_____
_____
_____
_____
_____
_____

Take Your Shot

Who can you intentionally share Jesus with this week using common language they can understand?

_____
_____
_____
_____
_____
_____
_____
_____

Day 24 – Great Balls of Fire!

Early one morning, when I was a teen, all the older men were up and the younger guys were still in bed. I vividly recall the sounds of the men talking and the smell of bacon cooking. I heard someone say, "Let's get that heater going." The 55-gallon drum wood-burning heater we had in our camp didn't put out much heat, but it was better than nothing. Someone else said, "I can't even light gas." Then my dad stated confidently, "I can!"

The next thing I heard was an explosion that shook the whole barn. Apparently, the fumes from the gas had built up. When my dad threw another match in there it spewed a fireball across the room, which exploded against the wall. That particular wall was where we had our gun rack holding fifteen guns, several boxes of shells and a large can of black powder. Guys threw their arms over their heads, dove behind furniture and rushed away from the fireball. Tommy Lewis never stopped stirring the eggs. All the teenagers quickly made our way into the kitchen. The men were slowly gathering themselves. Phil Ericson, normally unemotional, was cradling his can of black powder like a baby and saying in a traumatized high pitched voice, "This is black powder. It could have blown up. It could have blown up."

While we laugh about the fireball episode today, it could have had dire consequences. Thinking back through my life, there are so many times when I could have been killed. Think back through your own life and about how many close calls you have had. We're not guaranteed a tomorrow, so enjoy your life to the fullest and live for Jesus right now.

"Therefore, since we receive a kingdom which cannot be shaken, let us show gratitude, by which we may offer to God an acceptable service with reverence and awe; for our God is a consuming fire." Hebrews 12:28-29

Identify Your Target

When have you come close to dying?

Take Your Shot

How has that affected how you view life and how you live now?

Day 25 – There's More Than One Way to Bag a Buck

My Uncle Jerry has always been known as a big buck guy. We all know someone like him. Somehow, someway, he manages to hunt the same woods (or at least the edges of the same woods) that everyone else does, but he brings in a wall-hanger when everyone else only kills a doe or a basket rack. After asking around about how he did it I thought I had it figured out. Several guys told me, "He gets down and walks a lot. He stalks the big boys. That's why he gets them and others don't." I can't tell you how many wasted walks I took after hearing that. I guess I'm just not a good stalker.

As Uncle Jerry got older, his health slowed him down. Back surgery, brain surgery, and arthritis took their toll on him. Naturally, I thought he wouldn't be killing any more big bucks. A mixture of sadness for him and hope for me rose up inside of my selfish heart! But in the next couple of years he harvested two of the biggest deer we've ever gotten. He was now hunting strictly from a stand and my theory was ruined. He adjusted to his situation and continued to succeed.

There are different seasons in our walk with God. We can be successful in one way during a season of our life, and then have continued success in a totally different way later in life. We must always adapt to our circumstances as they change. If we remain obedient to following Jesus, He will keep using us for Kingdom work throughout our lives.

"There is an appointed time for everything. And there is a time for every event under heaven." Ecclesiastes 3:1

Identify Your Target

Have you ever had to adjust your walk with God from one method to another?

_____
_____
_____
_____
_____
_____
_____

Take Your Shot

Are there any areas in your life where you need to make adjustments to be more effective for the Kingdom today?

_____
_____
_____
_____
_____
_____
_____
_____

Day 26 – Iron Sharpens Iron

One of the best things about hunting is the friendships that you build. We have a community of guys who help each other build deer stands, make food plots, cut shooting lanes, clean deer, and everything else that needs to be done. The weird thing is that we laugh and enjoy all of that hard work together.

I learned a lot about hunting, guns, vehicles, careers, girls, God, food, and everything else guys discuss listening to the men around deer camp talking. From laughing at each other's mistakes to bragging about their glory days I heard their stories all the time. Without realizing it they were teaching me how to be a man.

I remember Tyge telling me when we were both 15-years-old how he wore his boots loose and not as many socks, so he could wiggle his toes. His feet would stay warmer that way. I taught him how to drive a standard transmission truck when we got older. With my dad gut-shooting so many deer we learned together how to follow a blood trail. Just talking to each other about things we saw and did helped make us better hunters.

Most guys don't have a friend close enough to talk to about spiritual things. It's an area we know is important, but most of us would rather handle things ourselves. We don't want to sound weak. It might not be easy to talk to someone about spiritual matters, but the Bible says over and over it's an important area for men. We get better at being followers of God, leaders in our homes, and the man God calls us to be when we have someone sharing that journey with us. Life is more productive and enjoyable together.

"He who walks with wise men will be wise, but the companion of fools will suffer harm." Proverbs 13:20

Identify Your Target

Who has been an inspiration to you in your spiritual life? Have you told them?

_____
_____
_____
_____
_____
_____
_____

Take Your Shot

How can you invest in someone else spiritually this week?

_____
_____
_____
_____
_____
_____
_____
_____

Day 27 – *This Is How We've Always Done It*

We have a deer stand that everyone loves. It's in a natural draw where deer funnel through. We've seen and harvested bucks and doe there for decades. It's produced morning, midday, and evening. We call it the Holly stand because the original stand was placed on a huge holly tree. Someone always hunts there, because you almost always see something. But a weird thing has recently happened. The land around the Holly stand was clear cut. Although the area within fifty yards of the stand looks exactly the same, beyond that there is a thicket surrounding it. Last season there wasn't a single deer seen from that heavily hunted stand. This year only one deer was spotted. The new terrain has changed the pattern of the deer. Even though the area immediately in the draw looks the same the deer are using another route.

Many churches have experienced this type of change. Programs that have worked for decades aren't producing results anymore. Things that God used in the past to reach the lost are no longer effective. Sometimes we have to accept that situations have changed and if we want to produce results for the Kingdom we might have to adjust what we're doing. Unfortunately, sometimes we care more about doing things the way they've always been done than we care about being effective for God.

I hunted in a different area this year on the days I normally would have been on the Holly stand. It wasn't easy, but I reminded myself that my purpose isn't to go hunt from a certain stand. My purpose when hunting is to try to harvest a deer. Know your purpose.

"To the weak I became weak, that I might win the weak; I have become all things to all men, so that I may by all means save some."
1 Corinthians 9:22

Identify Your Target

Are you are spending your time effectively for the Kingdom of God?

_____
_____
_____
_____
_____
_____
_____

Take Your Shot

What can you adjust to follow Jesus more efficiently?

_____
_____
_____
_____
_____
_____
_____
_____
_____

Day 28 – Everything Can Turn Around In Five Seconds

One season my dad was having a particularly bad year hunting. He had been out several times and not seen anything. Everyone else seemed to be seeing deer. If you've hunted long enough you have probably been through a drought like this. An older man listened to my dad and later caught him alone. He said, "I know it's frustrating not to see a deer, but remember this: it can all turn around in five seconds. A bad season can become the season of your life in just five seconds, if you just hang in there." Those words have been repeated many times when someone comes in frustrated at their lack of luck.

Most hunters have a story of getting ready to head back to camp when a deer suddenly showed up. John Honea had this happen to him one evening when he was hunting the Poison Ivy stand. Just as he was going to give up on another day of hunting, a huge eight-point stepped out and John got the big buck award that season. Had he left five seconds earlier, he would have gone home empty-handed.

In life there are seasons of highs and lows. Sometimes you're on top of the world and other times you're struggling through the valley of death. Patience is something we must have in our life. In our microwave world of having everything right now, God will sometimes make us wait to teach us to persevere. You may have to struggle through situations, but ultimately God will use it for your good. It's in your struggles where you will grow. No matter where you find yourself, remember that everything can turn around in five seconds if you keep going!

"And let endurance have its perfect result, so that you may be perfect and complete, lacking in nothing." James 1:4

Identify Your Target

Have you ever had to wait for something that you wanted immediately?

_____
_____
_____
_____
_____
_____
_____

Take Your Shot

What is something you are currently waiting on? How can you grow through this experience?

_____
_____
_____
_____
_____
_____
_____
_____

Day 29 – Same Event – Two Perspectives

One afternoon we went to cut shooting lanes around Guen Beard's Sparky #2 stand. It was a fairly new area we were hunting. When Guen builds a deer stand every board is flush and every corner is 90 degrees. It's far different than the Duncans who are known to "build and adjust."

We finished cutting the shooting lanes and my ten-year-old nephew, Cameron, was riding with me on our way back to camp. My dad was riding just ahead of us when all of a sudden he leaps off of his four-wheeler, grabs a big stick, and begins swinging crazily at a snake in the middle of the road. The snake slithers to the ditch, and my dad, wearing muck boots, kicks the evil black serpent back onto the road. He swings wildly with the stick repeatedly until he finally connects with snakes head, killing it. Dad holds his hands triumphantly in the air and asks, "What do you think about that?" I swelled with pride seeing my dad, whose DNA runs through my blood, kill the vicious snake. I was sure the ten year-old sitting in front of me was even more impressed. Cameron replied flatly, "It took you like 20 swings to hit it." Dad and I looked at each other and then busted out laughing.

Spiritually you may see or experience things that others totally miss. Sometimes it's because God only opens your eyes. Other times it's because you have been reading God's Word and are in tune with Him. If you want to know God and recognize where He is at work around you begin by simply telling him you want to know Him. No matter how far you have drifted, or even if you've never known Him, He's only a prayer away.

"Draw near to God and He will draw near to you. Cleanse your hands, you sinners; and purify your hearts, you double-minded." James 4:8

Identify Your Target

Has there ever been a time when you felt really close to God?

Take Your Shot

Spend some time intentionally drawing near to God and see what happens.

Day 30 – One Man's Trash Is another Man's... Deer Stand

As I sit in my deer stand writing this, I can look to my right and see where the slide used to be attached. There are bright yellow handles where kids could climb up a small rock wall to where I now sit waiting for a whitetail deer to come by. This was previously a playground-set in my sister's yard. I've seen deer stands made out of old playgrounds, plumbing tubing, and wooden pallets. In fact, one stand we built had a ladder made out of the white wrought-iron porch railing from my dad's house. It was truly an awful stand.

We put this particular stand up at noon one fall day next to a salt flat that was covered with hundreds of deer tracks. When my dad stepped on the porch railing ladder, the rung broke. Not one to give up easily he tried the next rung with the same result. After a third rung broke it was decided the stand was unsafe to hunt. That same afternoon between 3:30 and dark Dad, Uncle Jerry, and I all hunted on the ground beside that salt flat at different times. We never saw each other or knew anyone else had hunted there until that evening when we were eating supper. We laughed about all hunting it briefly that same afternoon and never seeing one another. The porch railing deer stand was eventually placed in the appropriate place...the trash.

In my walk with God I've had ideas that were treasures and others that were seemingly trash. But I've always learned something from trying to do things for Jesus. I believe that even when my attempts have been unsuccessful God has used them for a purpose. Sometimes that purpose is to teach me how to fail forward. Other times He's turned my trash into treasure. He doesn't waste an experience, even a bad one.

"And we know that God causes all things to work together for good to those who love God, to those who are called according to His purpose"
Romans 8:28

Identify Your Target

Have you ever felt like something you did was a failure?

_____
_____
_____
_____
_____
_____
_____
_____

Take Your Shot

What did you learn from that situation?

_____
_____
_____
_____
_____
_____
_____
_____

Day 31 – Homesick

I love going to deer camp. I always have. I get excited every time I get to make that trip to south Arkansas. In a lot of ways, I moved from boyhood to manhood down there. Deer season always seems to go way too fast. Some of the greatest memories in my life happened there. But as wonderful as deer camp is, it's always nice to come home.

I have a blast hunting, moving stands, eating, and laughing together with all the guys at camp. It's a variety of people and personalities that mesh into a great community. "Absence makes the heart grow fonder" is a common saying guys tell their wives during deer season. While it is usually said jokingly to justify going hunting, it is true. By the time I get back to my family, I'm always ready to see them.

The same is true in our relationship with Jesus. If you are a believer in Christ you should occasionally get homesick. This world is not our home. Jesus says plainly that he is going to prepare a place for us and he will come back to get us and take us there. It will be a place where there will be no more pain, sickness, or death. A place more wonderful than anything you can imagine. A place better than deer camp. I leave you with this question: Do you ever get homesick for heaven?

"For our citizenship is in heaven, from which also we eagerly wait for a Savior, the Lord Jesus Christ" Philippians 3:20

Identify Your Target

What things in this life do you wish were different?

_____
_____
_____
_____
_____
_____
_____
_____

Take Your Shot

How can you courageously take the responsibility to change the things you can change and accept the things you cannot control?

_____
_____
_____
_____
_____
_____
_____
_____
_____

A Note to the Reader about Salvation

We are all sinners in need of a Savior. The Bible says that every person has sinned (Romans 3:23). It goes on to say, while we don't deserve Salvation, God offers it to us as a free gift (Romans 6:23). In fact, while we were enemies of God and living in sin, God sent His only Son to die for us (Romans 5:8). We can receive eternal life with God by believing in His Son Jesus Christ (John 3:16). We show evidence of this faith in Jesus by believing in our hearts and confessing with our mouths that Jesus is Lord (Romans 10:9-10).

The very first thing we're supposed to do to when we are saved is to be baptized (Romans 6:4-5). The next step is fellowship with other believers and growing spiritually (Acts 2:42).

God loves you no matter how bad you think you are. You are not too far gone for Jesus to reach out and save you. Call out to God, turn from the direction you are going and follow Him.

You can do that right now in your own words if you like. If you need someone to talk with or are interested in learning more about what it means to have a relationship with Jesus Christ, a great resource is 1-888-Need-Him (1-888-633-3446), or on the web, go to www.needhim.org. You can also chat with someone about what a relationship with Jesus is all about at www.chataboutjesus.com. I pray you will acknowledge Jesus as your Lord and receive Salvation today!

Other Books by Brad Duncan

3t Challenge Series
First Fruits
Second Chances
Available on Amazon or Kindle

Free eBook
Jobe
Available on Kindle, iBooks, and most ebook readers

If you are interested in Brad speaking at your church or men's event, please contact him at www.3tchallenge.com or 3tchallenge@gmail.com.

Made in the USA
Las Vegas, NV
01 December 2022